A FRAGMENT

OF

ANCIENT EGYPTIAN ANNALS

(English translation of Ein Bruchstück Altägyptischer Annalen)

First English translation of a 1902 presentation about the Palermo Stone

by

DR. HEINRICH SCHÄFER

With contributions from

DR. LUDWIG BORCHARDT and PROFESSOR DR. KURT SETHE.

English translation

by

JOHN M. BUNKER
KAREN L. PRESSLER

Bunker Pressler Books

2023

A Fragment of Ancient Egyptian Annals
(English translation of Ein Bruchstück Altägyptischer Annalen)
First English translation of a 1902 presentation about the Palermo Stone by Dr. Heinrich Schäfer

ISBN: 979-8-9863571-1-9

Originally written in 1902 by Dr. Heinrich Schäfer

First English translation by
JOHN M. BUNKER AND KAREN L. PRESSLER

Bunker Pressler Books

"Two and a Guide"

Top cover: Palermo stone fitted with other fragments of the Royal Annals of Old Kingdom Egypt (Image: Lundström, 2010)

Questions regarding this book can be addressed to:

Bunker Pressler Books
8829 Heffelfinger Rd.
Churubusco, IN 46723

Email: Bunker.Pressler@gmail.com

Website:
<https://sites.google.com/site/edgarcayceandthehallofrecords/>

Presented at the General Session on March 6, 1902

[Reports of meetings St. XIII p. 255].

Submitted to press May 29, issued July 17, 1902.

ABBREVIATIONS LIST[1]

ÄZ.	*Zeitschrift für Ägyptische Sprache und Altertumskunde,* 78 vols. Leipzig, 1863-1943.
L. *D.*	R. Lepsius, *Denkmäler aus Ägypten und Äthiopien,* 6 vols. Berlin, 1849-58.
Mar. *Mast.*	A. MARIETTE, *Les Mastabas de l'Ancien Empire,* Paris, 1889.
Petr. *RT.* [Roy.]	W. M. F. Petrie, *The Royal Tombs of the Earliest Dynasties,* 2 vols. London (Egypt Exploration Fund) 1900-1.
Pyr.	K. SETHE, *Die Altägyptischen Pyramidentexte,* 4 vols. Leipzig, 1908-22, Also posthumously, *Übersetzung und Kommentar zu den Altägyptischen Pyramidentexten,* Gliickstadt-Hamburg, no date.
Rec. [de trav]	*Recueil de Travaux Relatifs à la philologie et à 0l'Archéologie Égyptiennes et Assyriennes,* 40 vols. Paris, 1870-1923.
R. *IH.*	E. DE ROUGE, *Inscriptions Hiéroglyphiques Copiés en Égypte,* 3 vols, in *Études Égyptologigues,* livraisons 9-11. Paris, 1877-8. The plates run consecutively, so that no volume number is quoted.
[*RT.*]	[See: PETR. *RT.*]

---

[1] [Added by translator for reference. Taken from Gardiner's *Egyptian Grammar.*]

1.

Since 1877, the Palermo Museum has housed a fragment of a strange inscription completely different from everything else known from Egypt. Because it includes some royal names from the early days of Egyptian history, the inscription has been mentioned several times since it became known. Especially in recent years it has come to the fore since the tombs of the kings from the first dynasties were found in Abydos.

Despite this, no satisfactory interpretation of the inscription as a whole has yet been given. The hitherto generally accepted view of its content has been formulated by Mr. E. Naville as follows[2]: "*Le document est une sorte de calendrier contenant le catalog des donations faites par un certain nombre de rois de l'Ancien-Empire et l' indieation de fetes a celebrer*"[3]. The following explanations are intended to show that this interpretation of the inscription does not do justice.

2.

The inscription was first published by Mr. A. Pellegrini in 1896, in a manner that was admirable considering its difficulty.[4] The new publication and arrangement hereby presented is based on a collation by L. Borchardt[5], while it is thanks to the kindness of Mr. A. Salinas in Palermo that we are able to reproduce his fine collotype photographs of the inscription here.

The inscription is on two sides of a 6.5 cm. thick slab of "Diorite anfibolica". The piece that has been preserved, which is 43.5 cm. high and 25 cm. wide in its greatest dimensions, has broken off on all sides and is only part of a large slab, the size of which we cannot even approximately determine.

One side of the fragment, which we shall call the obverse, concerns kings from the earliest times to the fourth dynasty, while the other side names those of the fifth dynasty. The inscription probably dates from the latter period. It is true that, as Borchardt has remarked and the

---

[2] *Rec. de trav.* XXI, p. 112

[3] [Translator's note: In English this reads: "The document is a kind of calendar containing the catalog of donations made by a certain number of kings of the Old Empire and the indication of festivals to be celebrated."]

[4] *Archivio storico Siciliano, Palermo* 1896, p. 297 ff. with two plates.

[5] L. Borchardt had made the detour to Palermo specifically to obtain a good copy of the inscription.

photograph confirms, the characters bear a distinctly Old Kingdom quality.

3.

When Sethe, Borchardt and I looked together at the photographs and collations Borchardt had brought with him in the autumn of 1901,[6] it became clear to us that one important fact had not been properly exploited up to now: the individual columns into which the writing strips on the stone are divided are separated by the sign for "year" 𓇳. The photograph shows quite clearly that it really is this sign.[7] From this it came to us as a natural conclusion that everything that follows such a 𓇳 until the next following one, refers to a year.[8] Now it has already been observed by Mr. Naville[9] that a larger series of such rubrics is always separated from the following ones by a line that goes beyond the line. Larger periods of time are marked here. That such a longer section represents the reign of a king is already probable from the names of the kings which are above the lines. But if you consider what Mr. Naville[10] has also noticed, namely that the marking of such a longer section is always immediately followed by the symbol 𓎤𓈖𓏏𓈇 "Unification of the two countries," which obviously refers to the coronation of the king, then the explanation of these sections as governments will be regarded as certain.

In and of itself it would now be possible for there to be nothing more in an inscription such as ours than the notation of some years marked by remarkable events, without a complete enumeration of all years being intended.

But such a thought is excluded in our inscription by the peculiar statement that is found at the end and at the beginning of each

---

[6] The following work offers essentially only the result of this joint discussion. It attempts to secure the basic features gained at that time for a more correct appreciation of the inscription, but only goes into details as far as the material immediately at hand allows.

[7] Mr. Naville mentions them with the words (p.115): *"The fact that these compartments are separated by palm leaves seems to me to indicate that they are birthdays, or feasts, or special days in which some event took place; where some ceremony was to be celebrated."* [Translated from the original French]

[8] On Mr. Pellegrini's tablets, the characteristic small dash has been forgotten everywhere.

[9] P.113 below *"quand le roi change."* [TRANSLATION: *"when the king changes"*.]

[10] Bottom of p.113 to top of p.114. Above all, the important reference is Eg. exemplar F. *The Temple of Deir El Bahari*, Plate 63 already quoted by him.

government section. In both places a number of months and days is regularly noted.

So it says, for example, under the first year of the reign of King U. (obverse, line 2, no. 3): ⟨hieroglyphs⟩. If this passage were to appear in a later Egyptian inscription as it is described here, one would never think of looking for a date in ⟨hieroglyphs⟩. We miss the usual indication of the season. But since it is to be explained as a date, Mr. Naville has used the exact corresponding inscription from *Der el bahri* (Eg. Expl. F. *Der el bahri,* Plate 63) , which has ⟨hieroglyphs⟩ in place of it. So Mr. Naville rightly comments on the dates of our stone: *One could conclude from these dates that in those remote times all the months were counted in a row without worrying about the division into seasons, which, perhaps, had not yet been adopted.*[11] The inscription from *Der el bahri* proves by the words ⟨hieroglyphs⟩ "beginning of happy years",[12] which it adds to the date, what actually goes without saying, that this date is the first day of the king's government.

Now, however, Mr. Naville has applied the same explanation to the monthly and daily data at the end of the governments. If, for example, in the last part of the year under King T. (obverse, line 2, no. 2) it says: ⟨hieroglyphs⟩, he also translates this as a date: 6th month, 7th day. But it does not seem possible to me to treat these end notations in the same way as the opening notations. They are certainly not data. What date should be mentioned here, at the end of every government? The only thing one could think of would be the day of the king's death. But its regular notation would be of no practical value, especially if, as we have just seen, the date of the first day of the new king is given. In general, the two dates should not differ, since the new king reckoned his reign directly from the death of the old one.

If one looks more closely, one notices that in the inscription the months at the beginning and at the end of the governments are treated quite differently. While the date of the accession to power is nested together with the other events in a yearly section, as is proper, a special yearly section is always devoted to the months and days noted at the end of the governments. This is totally inconsistent with the assumption of a

---

[11] [Translator's note: Translated from the French.]
[12] According to Sethe's correct translation ÄZ., XXXVI, p. 66.

date. On the contrary, I think it can be concluded with complete certainty that these final statements do indeed mean independent years but not complete. Where there is such a statement, and this will always be the case, the king did not complete his last year, but only, for example, 6 months and 7 days.

Such an indication of the months and days comprising the unfinished last years would be useless if the preceding rubrics represented only a selection of the years of the king's reign concerned. Rather, the years enumerated must follow one another without gaps, so that if the list were preserved in full, the number of years, months, and days reigned by each of the kings mentioned could easily be deduced.

But I think we can go further. What sense would there be in the careful noting of every single, even incomplete, year of government, if not because the purpose of the inscription had demanded such exact noting of time? In my opinion, it follows from this meticulous precision that the governments have again formed an unbroken line among themselves. If the stone had come down to us in its entirety, we would find recorded on it every single year of Egyptian history, from the earliest times to the fifth dynasty. That means: in the Palermo Stone we have before us a fragment of official Egyptian annals.

This agrees well with an observation that Mr. Naville has already made. As one can see, even without examining the content more closely, the character of the notation changes within the inscription.

The first line of the obverse contains only the names of kings of Lower Egypt without indicating any years. The second through fifth lines of the obverse, corresponding to the first three dynasties, enumerate the individual years, but only using certain main events. In the sixth line, which concerns the reign of Snefru, from the beginning of the fourth dynasty, the tidings flow more plentifully: the annual divisions are twice or three times as wide as in the preceding lines. On the reverse, which deals with the Fifth Dynasty, the information is even more detailed and the range of years increases up to ten times that of the obverse. The closer you got to your own time, the more you could and wanted to report.

Whoever surveys the facts just enumerated will be convinced that the explanation of the inscription as a fragment of annals is inevitable. The existence of such annals is always to be assumed in a cultural people that does not yet have an era, and, as we shall see below, the regent years have not yet been counted; but it is the first time that a fragment of the same can be found among the Egyptian monuments that have come down to us. The well-known Turin royal papyrus, which only notes the sum of the years for each king, albeit also with details of the excess months and days, is only an excerpt from such annals.[13] The lists of kings otherwise preserved in the inscriptions are again only extracts from lists like the papyrus at Turin. They only give the names of the kings, and these not even fully.

4.

Even if it comes as no surprise to us that in the fifth dynasty people still knew about the fourth dynasty, which had to remain in the memory of the people because of its large buildings, one could still be surprised how a tradition could be preserved, which, from the times of the first dynasties, had to indicate a specific event for each year of a king.

Here an observation of Sethe's comes in, which explains this marvel very naturally, and not only confirms my interpretation of the Palermo Stone, but is also of far-reaching importance for the history of Old Kingdom Egypt.

Sethe points out that in other inscriptions a whole series of dates has been preserved in which the years are not named with numbers, but after certain events. Sethe himself will probably explain his discovery elsewhere. Of the examples he gave us, I would like to mention only a few that contribute most to the explanation of our inscription.

1. "Year of the struggle and defeat of the northern peoples" on the vessel of King (3rd dynasty) found in Hierakonpolis.

2. "Year of Worship of Horus" on a tablet from the tomb of King in Abydos: Petrie, Royal tombs I, plate 12, no.1; II, plates 8, 5. Similarly, under the king , Petrie I, plate 17, no. 29, under , Petrie II, plate 39, no. 54.

3. "Year of the second census of all large and small livestock of the North and South", LD. II, 116a in an

---

[13] Manetho also noted at least the excess months in his historical work, as the fragment preserved by Josephus shows.

inscription by Phiops II in Wadi Marara. Another similar inscription from Wadi Marara, but from the time of 'Issi, ÄZ, 1869, p. 26 (incorrect).

I myself would like to add:

4. ⟨hieroglyphs⟩ in the very old inscription of the Berlin collection No. 14467:[14] "Year of the union of the two countries, month 4 of the harvest season, day 4".

As Sethe remarks, these dates are based on data which correspond exactly to those on the Palermo Stone. Compare for example:

With 1: ⟨hieroglyphs⟩ "the year of the defeat of the Inw" in obverse, line 3, as well as the Negro campaign under Snefru in line 6;

With 2: ⟨hieroglyphs⟩ "the year of worship of the god Horus". This indication is found on the kings of the second, fourth and fifth rows on the obverse. According to Sethe's guess, which was correct, it designates a journey to Hierakonpolis in Upper Egypt, in order to perform a cult act there, as the ancient kings of Upper Egypt before Menes did, according to Sethe the so-called ⟨hieroglyphs⟩ "the worshipers of Horus", did. The trip takes place every two years;

With 3: ⟨hieroglyphs⟩ "Year of the second count of the cattle" is in the second line of the back of our inscription, while line 5 of the obverse says twice that "the gold and the field" was counted ox ⟨hieroglyphs⟩, while the cattle are not mentioned. Much more frequent, however, are statements of the form: "Year of the second (third, etc.) time of counting" without specifying what was counted. Such a note is found regularly every two years in the kings of the fourth and fifth rows on the obverse, while in Snefru it is also counted once in two consecutive years.

They are either[15] censuses of financial property or censuses of private property for tax purposes, usually covering the whole, but sometimes

---

[14] Egypt. inscription p.71.

[15] Compare the inscription of Weni, line 36 ⟨hieroglyphs⟩ and many other allusions to this in other texts. As Weni indicates, this count sometimes extended to the drudgery to be performed. However, as Borchardt notes, the intervals of the counts seem somewhat small for counts of the total national wealth, but this is not a serious obstacle. Incidentally, Borchardt draws attention to the fact that from the "census maps" Griffith,

extending only to livestock or land or cash. At the end of the back there is another abbreviation. It just says ⌐⊙' ı ı "year of the fifth time". Certainly this is also related to the censuses;

With 4: the note ⬧ *sma tawi*, which, as mentioned above, is always found on our stone in the first year of every king.

Thus, Sethe is undoubtedly right to claim that the events mentioned on our stone behind the ⌐ characters are those used to describe the individual years of the reign.[16]

It will occur to anyone who has followed us this far that exactly the same custom of dating by event is found in Babylonia in the same ancient period. For comparison, a passage from the Old Babylonian Annals is included here, thanks to the kindness of Mr. Messerschmidt for the translation. It is the beginning of King *Bur-Sin's* reign:

Year in which Bur-Sin (became) king.
Year in which the king destroyed Bur-Sin Urbillum.
Year in which he made the throne of the god Bel.
Year in which he raised the exalted, great Lord (i.e. a priest) of the god Anu (and) established the lord (priest) of the god Nannar.

Kahun, Pap. 9 and 10 (household census cards), 21 (land census card) and 16/17 (livestock census card?) for the middle empire really such general counts can be proven, and since for this time an interval of 14 years seems to result, which was still recorded in the Greek and Roman times (see Wilcken, *Ostraka*, p. 438), until the indictions with their fifteen-year intervals were introduced.

[16] Such dating according to events is very common in ordinary life among all peoples. Mr. Spiegelberg points me to such an example from an Egyptian text that he quotes in his "Studies and Materials," pp. 87ff. has published: During an interrogation, a woman is asked about the whereabouts of a sum of money. She replies: "I used it to buy grain in the year of ... animals (some rodents) when there was starvation." This explains why it remained sterile when Mr. Naville in his most recent essay (Rec. XXIV, 118 after Maspero) correctly picked up the inscription of the BS vessel, when Sethe had long been aware of some of the inscriptions discussed above, for example, recognized the BS inscription and the naming of the cattle counts in the rock inscriptions of *Wadi Marara* as dates, and even though I read the inscription Berlin 14467 *rnpt sma tawi* and related it to the first year of a king; it was only through Sethe when we were dealing with the Palermo stone that everything was put in the right light. Because it is precisely the knowledge of the official and continuous use of this type of dating in ancient Egypt that is at issue here.

Year in which he installed the lord (priest) of the great abode of the goddess Nana.

Year in which he destroyed the city of Shashru.

etc. etc.

The resemblance of our Egyptian inscription to these Babylonian annals is striking.

5.

In order to understand the practical use of such a dating method, I would like to draw your attention to the following:

In the first place, of course, two years within the same government could never bear the same designation, as such repetition would cause great confusion. In fact, it is never the case on our stone either. For example, so many annual notes also start with *sms Hr* or *Ha stni ha biti*, that they are all differentiated by further additions.

Secondly, every year could not, from its very first day, bear a designation after an event. Only when a characteristic event had occurred, or even after the end of the year, could an official decree be issued that named the year. In the meantime, people helped each other in a very obvious way. For example, in the Babylonian annals, the second year of King Bur-Sin is referred to as "the year in which King Bur-Sin destroyed the city of Ur-billum". In the documents from that year, on the other hand, there is also the naming: "Year after when Bur-Sin became king." Apparently, the official name of the year had not yet become known to the writer of the document.

That the Egyptians proceeded in exactly the same way is shown, for example, by the dates of rock inscriptions of the Old Kingdom in the Wadi Marära. So dates an inscription from the time of King *Phiops I*:[17]

𓍶 𓅃 𓂝 𓊖 𓈖 𓏤𓏤𓏤𓏤 𓍿 𓈖𓈖𓈖 ☉ 𓏤𓏤

---

[17] LD.II 116, with improvement of first ☉ in 🜨 . – The almost contemporary inscription

LD.II 115*g* shows the form 𓍶 𓂝 𓊖 𓈖 𓏤𓏤𓏤𓏤𓏤𓏤𓏤 𓈖𓈖 ☉𓏤𓏤𓏤𓏤𓏤. The

writer of LD.II 115*k* only gives 𓍶 ⊗ 𓂝, i.e. only "year after", and forgets the most important thing, namely "the eighteenth time (of the count)", LD. II 115*k* and 115*g* are both, by the way, from the same year.

"in the year after the 18th time (counting) in the third month of the harvest season on the 8th day."

In Babylonia as well as in Egypt it happened that some years never received their own name, but were given in the annals in the form "year after that in which...". Such cases are frequent in the Babylonian annals, but they are also to be found on our Egyptian fragment, if the assumption is correct, that in line 3, no. 1 on the reverse ⌐ ⌐ | | is to be read "year after the second time (of counting)"[18] after the second time (of counting)"[18]

Even if a year only really got its own official name after an event towards the end, confusion could never arise from such auxiliary designations.

6.

Finally, for the general understanding of the stone, we have to discuss a remarkable part of its inscriptions. Under the individual sections of the year there are regular notations giving a measure in cubits, without it being clear what they are about. In the second line of the obverse, which dates back to an ancient time, the indication is completely missing for two years; from then on, it is no longer missing in any year. Furthermore, as Mr. Erman observed, the indications of the various lines and times are not given with the same precision. The first four lines of the obverse give these measurements only in cubits ⌐▭, spans ⌐[19], palmwidths ▦,

and fingers ‖, while the fifth and sixth lines of obverse and reverse still use even fractions of fingers.[20] These later parts therefore have a more precise method of measurement than the older ones.

What do these cubits mean? They must surely be something important, otherwise they would not have been officially preserved. Hence the interpretation proposed by Borchardt that they are heights of the Nile, seems very plausible. Knowing the height of the Nile in the

---

[18] Similar in Line 4, No. 1.

[19] Mr. Erman points out the striking fact that in our inscription this measure is restricted to lines 2 and 3 of the obverse only and is never accompanied by palms and fingers. — The sign itself clearly shows the tensely placed hand, with the single line indicating the thumb and the double line the other fingers. In later times this character, whose phonetic value we do not know, is thrown together with the bird's claw ⌐, which can probably be read 8 t.

[20] ⌐ is ½, ⌐ is certainly ⅔; but what ⌐ is, I do not know; is it about ¾?

individual years was of interest to the state even years later because of the taxes. This interpretation is certainly correct, but it is not as straightforward as it may appear at first glance.

The numbers do not move at a level that we are used to finding with Nile height information, but only lie between 1 and 8 cubits. The dimensions of the stone must therefore be measured from a far higher point than the lowest summer low, which is otherwise regarded as zero. So it would actually be necessary to add a specific, unknown number to all the cubit numbers mentioned on our stone. Although no other method of this kind is known to us for measuring the height of the Nile, this assumption lacks any serious difficulties.[21]

In the following I give the text of the inscription, taking into account the photographs of Mr. Salinas and Borchardt's collation, broken down into the individual years. The translation attached is, of course, only an attempt, and even the occasional remarks given cannot claim to exhaust so difficult a text. That much of what has been said is questionable, even where it is not expressly said, always remains to be considered. But such an attempt at translation is the best means of making it possible to understand the inscription as a whole, and that is all that matters to us for the time being.

---

[21] Borchardt himself expresses a small concern, that is the accuracy, which is almost excessive for water level measurements, which even distinguishes between $^2/_3$ and $^3/_4$ fingers. Mr. Erman has finally observed that if these elevations are averaged for each line, these averages decrease from line to line. I wish only to state this observation here, without attempting an explanation of the fact.

Kings of Lower Egypt
from before unification
of the two countries.

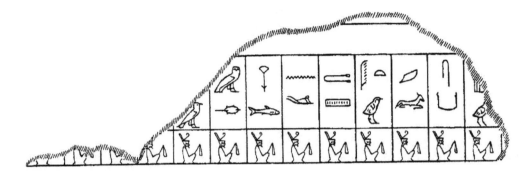

The names could be rewritten as:

1.---pw,   4. Tiw,   7. Wad-and,
2 ska,   5. Ts,   8. Mh,
3. Ha-iw,   6. N-hb (?)   9. -------
                  10. – 13. destroyed.

Apparently we only have kings of Lower Egypt here, from the time when the two kingdoms were still separate. Whether the kings of Upper Egypt also stood on our stone cannot be said. If the memorial stone comes from a temple in Lower Egypt, it is possible that the kings of Upper Egypt were not mentioned at all. In any case, it is impossible that such names of kings from Abydos can be found under these names, as Spiegelberg (ÄZ. 35, p. 10) hoped.

As the free strip above the name shows, the series probably had a summary title.

The blank stripe in the uppermost corner of the stone probably belongs to the edge.

King T. **Name not received.**
Year Worship of Horus.[1]
X+1 Birth of Anubis.[2]

> [1]See introduction §4. The festival is only
> mentioned in lines 2-5 of the obverse.
> [2]Also found on the tablets of dynasty I,
> example Petrie, Roy. I. II Plate Xl, 1.

No Nile height yet.

[Obverse]
Line 2
No 1.

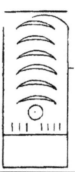

Year 6 months, 7 days.
X+2 Incomplete year.

No. 2.

King U. **Name not received.**
Year 1. Fourth month, day 13.[1]
Unification of the two countries.[2]
Moving around the wall.

> [1]See introduction §3.
> [2]See introduction §4.

Height of the Nile: 6 cubits.

No. 3.

[Obverse]

[King U.]   [Line 2.]

Year 2. Worship of Horus.[1]   No. 4.

Festival of the *tesher*.[2]

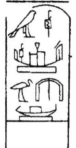

[1]The festival is now celebrated every two years.
[2]The ship is probably only a determinative,
see line 2 No. II.

Nile Height: Not specified.

Year 3. Birth of the two children of King of Lower   No. 5.
Egypt.[1]

[1]These deities come e.g. Pyr. T.79=M.109=
N.22 ago.

Height of the Nile: 4 cubits, 1 hand.

Year 4. Worship of Horus.   No. 6.
-----------------------[1]

[1]This second part is completely incomprehen-
sible to me. Sethe comments; The first character
looks like the later form of *kap* "to smoke"; the
second, which seems to represent a bird severed
by a knife, recalls the well-known determinative of
hsk "to behead" in the pyramid texts;
finally, the third sign seems to represent a woman wounded or beaten.

Nile height: 5 cubits, 5 hands, 1 finger.

14

[King U.]

Year 5. Plan (?) of the house *Khsf-ntrw.*[1]
Festival of *Sokaris* (?).

No. 7

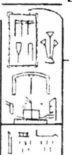

> This must denote an action preceding
> "stretching the rope." Compare Line 3, No.6.
> The building itself will be the king's palace
> or tomb. The battlements are not entirely
> secure.

Nile height: 5 cubits, 5 hands, 1 finger.

Year 6. Worship of Horus.
Birth of the goddess *Iamt.*[1]

No. 8.

> [1]A goddess often mentioned in the Old
> Kingdom, e.g. Pyr. T.76 – M.230 =
> W.197 - N.608 Mar. Mast. A.1 = R.I.H. 98.

Nile height: 5 cubits, 1 hand.

Year 7. Appearance of the King of Upper Egypt.
Birth of Min.

No. 9.

Height of the Nile: 5 cubits.

Year 8. Worship of Horus.
Birth of Anubis.

No. 10

Nile height: 6 cubits, 1 hand.

[King U.]  [Line 2.]

Year 9. I. Time of the celebration of the *Dt*-festival. No. 11

The ship is only a determinative, probably like that in line 2 no. 4.

Nile Height: 4 cubits, 1 span.

Year 10. Destroyed. 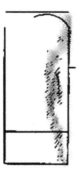 No. 12

As it is certainly to be assumed that the king's name stood above the middle of his reign, at least 10 (the number of years preserved) + 6 (the space required by the name) = 16 years are missing from the reign of King U here. Line 4 shows that the names of kings were not at the beginning of the sections, and line 3 shows that they were not at the end. So this king reigned for at least 26 years.

King V. **Name not preserved.** Just the name of his mother[1]: **Line 3.**

----*rt*

[1]The woman's name can hardly be explained otherwise at this point.

Using the same reasoning as in line 2, at least 13 (the number of preserved years behind the name) +5 (space for the name) = 18 years missing at the beginning.

16

[King V]

Year Stay in *Hka* - - - and in the Temple of *Saw*[1]   No. 1

X+1   [1] The translation, especially "stay," is only a guess. Prepositions are often absent from these ancient texts. We do not know where the two cities are

located. Similar use of 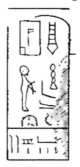 on the dating tablets, e.g. Petrie, *Roy.* I. II Plate X. 2 (Sethe).

Nile height: 3 cubits, 1 hand, 2 fingers.

Year Hitting the *'inw*.[1]   No. 2

X+2   [1] So a campaign against the tribes between Egypt and the Red Sea,

Nile Height: 4 cubits, 1 span.

Year   Appearance of the King of Upper Egypt.   No. 3

X+3   Appearance of the King of Lower Egypt.
        Sd-Festival

Nile height: 8 cubits, 3 fingers.

Year   .... the districts (lakes?) of the west,   No. 4

X+4   All people.

    The translation is very questionable.

    A verb is missing, or is it in ?

Height of the Nile: 3 cubits, 1 span.

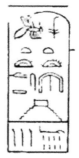

[King V]

Year 2nd time of the *Dt*-festival.
X+5 The festival is thus repeated at longer intervals
not known to us.

Height of the Nile: 5 cubits, 2 hands.

Year Plans (?) of the house "Seats of the Gods."
X+6 Festival of Sokaris.

The foundation for this building was laid
in the following year.

Nile height: 5 cubits, 1 hand, 2 fingers.

No. 6

Year Tightening the Cord for the House
X+7 "Seats of the Gods" by the Priest[1]
of the *Sshat*.
Great Thor.[2]

[1] according to the old usage instead of
(Sethe).

[2] This is also found on the slate of
Hierakonpolis ÄZ. 36, Plate 12 (Naville).

Nile Height: 4 cubits, 2 hands.

No. 7

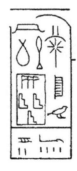

18

[King V.]

Year x+8. Opening (?) of the lake from the house of the "Seat of the Gods".[1]
Crooked Hippopotamus.

No. 8

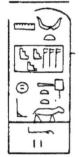

[1]Probably the sacred lake of the temple.

Height of the Nile: 2 cubits.

Year x+9. Stay in Herakleopolis and on the lake of the temple of the god *Ari-sf*(?).

No. 9.

For "stay" see the comment on Line 3 No. I. This form of the temple is common in the oldest inscriptions (cf. ÄZ. 34 p. 160; Petrie, *Royal Tombs II*, plate X and more).

Height of the Nile: 5 cubits.

Year x + 10. Trip to *Sah*(?) *stni* and *Wr-k3-* ....

No. 10

"Travel at night" is very questionable. One thinks of *khd*. The preposition, like
𐦀 and otherwise, would not be written.

Height of the Nile: 4 cubits, ı span.

Year x + 11. Year Birth of the God *Sd*.[1]

No. 11

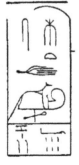

[1]The name of this god 𓂧𓄿 comes before Mar. Mast. D 19 (p. 229) and in the name 𓂧𓄿 (Sethe).

Nile: 6 cubits, 1 hand, 2 fingers.

[King V.]

Year   Appearance of the King of Lower Egypt.

x + 12.   First time walking around (?) the Apis.[1]

No. 12

> [1] As with most of the ones mentioned in our inscription, we do not know what kind of ceremony this is. Since, according to Manetho, the Apis cult was introduced under Kaiechos, we are here in the second dynasty.

Height of the Nile: 2 cubits, 1 span.

Year

x+13.   Birth of the *Sshat* and the *Mafdt*.

No. 13.

> The cat (?) on the ⸮ is also often the determinative of this goddess name (cf. e.g. Petrie, *Royal Tombs II*, Plate VII).

Nile Height: 3 cubits, 5 hands, 2 fingers.

Year   [appearance of] king of Upper Egypt.

x+14.   Birth [--------].

No. 14.

This king reigned for at least 32 years.

King *Ntrn*. **King *Ntrn*, the son of *Nb* ----.**

This is interpreted according to Sethe, who recognizes in ⌐ᵒ‿‿ the word *rn* "child," which he dealt with in *Garstang Biet Khallaf* (on K. 1, 3a).

We had already assumed above in point 3 that the names of the mothers were given for the kings.

Ntrn is the king whose name is among others on the shoulder of the Cairo No. 1 statue and which occurs in Abydos.

Since in this government the censuses take place regularly every two years, the year x + 1 will be the 5th or 6th of the king.

Year	Worship of Horus.[1]	No. 1
x+1	[3rd time of the count.][2]	

    [1] The "worshipping of Horus" reappearing here was missing entirely in the previous line.
    [2] The dating by census begins with this line.

Nile Height: Destroyed.

Year	Appearance of the King of Upper Egypt.	No. 2.
x+2	Tightening the rope over the house of *Hor-Ra.*	

Nile height: 3 cubits, 4 hands, 2 fingers.

[King Ntrn]

Year	Worship of Horus.	No. 3.
x+3	4th time of the count.	

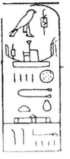

Height of the Nile: 4 cubits, 2 fingers.

Year	Appearance of the King of Upper Egypt.	No. 4.
x+4.	Appearance of the King of Lower Egypt.	
	Walking around Apis.	

Nile height: 4 cubits, 1 hand, 2 fingers

Year	Worship of Horus.	No.5.
x+5.	5th time of the count.	

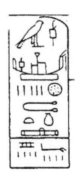

Height of the Nile: 4 cubits, 4 hands.

Year	Appearance of the King of Lower Egypt.	No. 6.
x+6.	2nd time of the Sokaris festival.[1]	

[1]This festival is also repeated at certain longer
  intervals. Until the next time in line 4 No.12 it
  is 6 years.

Nile Height: 3 cubits, 4 hands, 2 fingers.

[King Ntrn]

Year Worship of Horus.
x+7. 6th time of the count.

Height of the Nile: 4 cubits, 3 fingers.

No. 7.

Year 1st time of festival *Dwa-Hr-pt.*[1]
X+8 Settlement of the cities "*Shm-Rea*"
and "North House".

> The festival and the cities are otherwise
> unknown.
> [1]According to Sethe: "Worship of Horus from
> heaven."

Height of the Nile: 4 cubits, 3 fingers.

No. 8

Year Worship of Horus.
x+9. 7th time of the count.

Nile height: 1 cubit.

No. 9

Year The appearance of the king of Lower
x+10 Egypt.
2nd time of running around Apis.

Nile height: 3 cubits, 4 hands, 3 fingers

No. 10

[King Ntrn]

Year	Worship of Horus.	No. 11
x+11	8th time of the count.	

Nile Height: 3 cubits, 5 hands, 2 fingers.

Year	Appearance of the king of Lower Egypt.	No. 12
x + 12.	3rd time of the Sokaris Festival.[1]	

[1] Comparison to line 4 no. 6.

Height of the Nile: 2 cubits, 2 fingers.

Year	Worship of Horus.	No. 13
x+13.	9th time of the count.	

Height of the Nile: 2 cubits, 2 fingers.

Year	Appearance of the king of Lower Egypt.	No. 14
X+14	Sacrifice(?)...Goddess Nhbt... Dt-Fest.[1]	

[1]The translation is very uncertain.

Height of the Nile: 3 cubits.

24

[King Ntrn.] [Line 4.]

Year   Worship of Horus. No. 15
x+15. 10th time of the count.

     Nile Height: Destroyed.

Year   Destroyed. No. 16
X+16

     Nile Height: Destroyed.

At least 15 more years of the king are missing, so that he reigned at least 35 years.

King W. **Name not preserved.** **Line 5**
     Judging by the "counts," 10 or 11 years are missing at the beginning.

Year   Worship of Horus. No. 1
x+1. 6th time of the count.

     Nile Height: 2 cubits, 4 hands, 1 $^1/_2$ fingers.

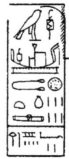

[King W]

Year   Appearance of the King of Upper Egypt.

x + 2.   Appearance of the King of Lower Egypt.
The *Mn-Ntrt* building is made of stones.

Nile height: 2 cubits, 3 hands, 1 finger.

No. 2

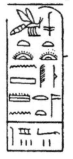

Year   Worship of Horus.

x+3.   7th counting of the gold and fields.[1]

[1] See introduction § 4.

Nile height: 3 $^2/_3$ cubits.

No. 3

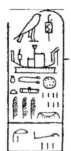

Year   Worship of Horus.

x+4.   Birth of *Kha-skhmwi*.[1]

[1] Correctly Naville. It is the king known from Abydos.

Height of the Nile: 2 cubits, 6 hands, 24 fingers.

No. 4

Year   Worship of Horus.

x+5.   8th counting of the gold and fields.

Nile Height: 4 cubits, 2 hands, 2$^2/_3$ fingers

No. 5

26

[King W]

Year 4th time of bringing the wall from *Dwa Dfa*.[1]

x+6. Shipbuilding (?).[2]

[1] I don't know what that means.
[2] See the comment on line 6 no.2.

Height of the Nile: 4 cubits, 2 hands.

Year 2 months, 23 days. No. 7

x+7 This incomplete year is crammed into one rubric
with the first of the new king. Apparently there
was an oversight here that was noticed only later.

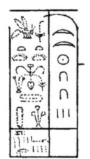

So this king reigned for a total of 16 or 17 years, 2 months, 23
days.

King X

Year 1. Name not preserved.

Appearance of the king of Upper Egypt.
Appearance of the King of Lower Egypt.
Union of the two countries.[1]
Moving around the wall.

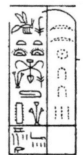

[1] See introduction. The date (see line 2 no.3) is
missing here. It is also not absolute for the use
of the annals essential.

Height of the Nile: 4 cubits, 2 hands, $2^2/_3$
fingers.

[King X]

Year 2. Appearance of the king of Upper Egypt.
Appearance of the King of Lower Egypt.
Introduction[1] of the King to the both *Snwi*
houses.[2]

No. 9

> [1] Naville. Instead of the fish there seems to be a
> knife.
> [2] Sethe. Are the determinatives two steles?

Height of the Nile: 4 cubits, 12/3 hands.

Year 3. Worship of Horus.
Birth of Min.

No. 10

Nile Height: 2 cubits, 3 hands, 2 ¾ fingers

Year 4. Appearance of the King of Upper Egypt
Appearance of the King of Lower Egypt.
Tightening the cord for the *Kbh-ntrw*
building.

No. 11

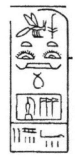

Nile Height: 3 cubits, 3 hands, 2 fingers.

Year 5. Worship of Horus.

Height of the Nile: 3 cubits ---.

No. 12

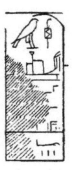

At least 5+6 years are still missing here, so that this

king reigned for at least 16 years.

King Sneferu. The heading was not preserved, but the name is **Line 6.**
evident from the years. There are 10 or 11 years
missing at the beginning, as can be seen from the
"censuses" (if these took place every second year,
cf. line 6 no. 4).

Year -------- **No. 1**
x+1.   Birth of the two children of the king from
Lower Egypt.[1]
[6. time of the count?]

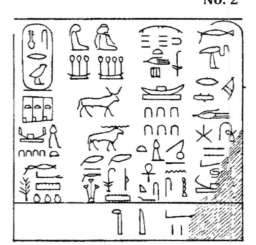

   [1] Compare line 2 no. 5.

Nile Height: Destroyed.

Year **No. 2**
x +2.   Construction of --- one-
hundred-foot *Dwa-tawi*
ships from *Mr*[1]-wood and
60 sixteen-foot king
barges.[2]
Chopping up the negro
country. Bringing 7,000
prisoners, men and
women, as well as 200,000
head of cattle and small
livestock.
Building the wall of the
south and north country
with names (?): Houses of
Snfrw.

[King Snefru.]

Bringing 40 ships made of (?) cedar wood.

[1]The relation of *shd dshr* to shipbuilding is evident for example, from the appendix to an account of shipbuilding in Petrie, *Medum,* Plate XI.

Ships made of this wood, which was still used in the New Kingdom for the same purposes as cedar wood, also appear on the tablets from Abydos (Petrie, roy. t. II, plate X.).

[2] compare ship 8 of Uni (line 41).

Height of the Nile: 2 cubits, 2 fingers.

Year x+3.	Making 35 ---- 122 cattle Construction of a 100-cell *Dw3-t3wi* ship made of cedar wood and two 100-cell ships made of *Mr*-wood. 7th time of the count. Nile height: 5 cubits, 1 hand, 1	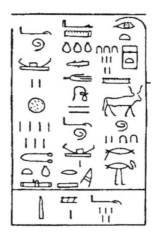 **No. 3**

Year x+4.	Erecting [of the buildings] "High is the crown of Snefru on the southern gate" and "High is the crown of Snefru on the northern gate." Manufacture of the doors to the royal palace made of cedar. 8th time of the count. This is the first time the census occurs in two consecutive years.	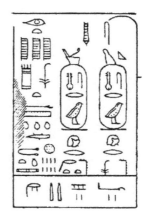 **No. 4**

Nile Height: 2 cubits, 2 hands, 2 ¾ fingers.

30

[King Snefru.]
Year   Destroyed.
x+5

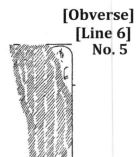

[Obverse]
[Line 6]
No. 5

Nile Height: Destroyed.

King Y.   **Line 7**

Only a small fragment of the header, ending with his mother's name, survives from his government:

Whether line 7 was the last line on the front, or whether others followed, cannot be determined.

King Z. (Menkaure?).   Name not preserved.

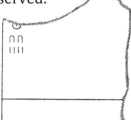

Reverse
Line 1
No. 1.

Year x.

[--- months] 24 days.

It is, of course, the king's last incomplete year again. Why the space in front of the number is blank seems inexplicable to me.

King Shepseskaf. Headline not preserved, but name to be
Year deduced from yearly note. **No. 2**
1

The rest broken off

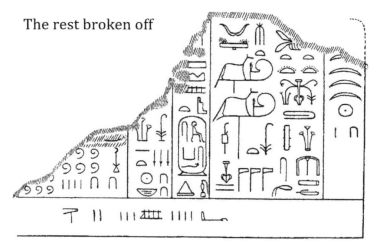

a) 4+x^th month, 11th day.
b) Appearance of the King of Upper Egypt, appearance
the king of Lower Egypt. Unification of the two
countries. Moving around the wall. *Sshd* festival. Birth
of the two *Wp-wa-wt.* The king worships the gods that
have united the two countries.[1]
c) ------------- Choice of place to pyramid *Kbh-Shpsskaf.*[2]
d) ------------- North and South. 20 ---all days
e) ------- 1624 ---- 600 ---

[1] Are the gods designated by this, whose standards so often appear
be carried to the king?
[2] So the king really begins right away in his first year with the
construction of his tomb.

Nile height: 4 cubits, 3 hands, 2 ½ fingers.

King Weserkaf. **Line 2**

Header not preserved, but name to be deduced from
yearly note.
If the censuses took place every two years, four or five
years are missing at the beginning.

32

[King Weserkaf.]

Year   3rd time of finding (?) ------
x+1.

No. 1

Nile Height: Destroyed.

Year
X+2   No. 2

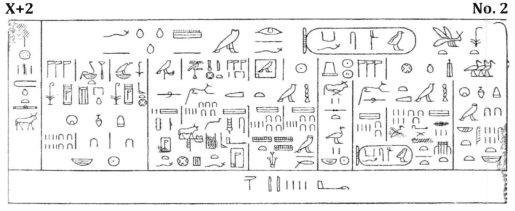

a) The king of Upper and Lower Egypt *Wsr-kaf* donated as his memorial to:
    Spirits of Heliopolis ... : 20 sacrificial rations at each ---- festival
                           36 acres of farmland[1] --- in --- land of *Wsr-kaf*
    Gods of the sun
        sanctuary *Sp-Rea* ... : 24 acres of farmland --- in the ---land of *Wsr-kaf*
                           2 oxen and 2 geese every day
    Rea .... : 44 acres of farmland in the districts of the north country
    Hathor .....…............. : 44 acres of farmland in the districts of the north country
    Gods of the house of Horus
        of *Dba-khrw(?)t*[2] ... : 54 acres of farmland. Setting up the chapel of his
                           (Horus) Temple at Buto in the *Xoitic Gau*
    Spa .... : 2 acres of farmland. construction of his temple
    Nkhbt in the *Ntri*
        (house) of the south : 10 sacrificial rations daily

[King Weserkaf.]

> Buto in *Pr-nw* .... : 10 sacrificial rations daily
> Gods in the *Ntri* (house)
>   of the south .... : 48 sacrificial rations daily

....

  b) 3rd time payment of cattle.

> [1]The word "tomorrow" is always meant to indicate only that crops will follow.
> [2]So according to Sethe, also reading *ntri* below.

Height of the Nile: 4 cubits, 2 ½ fingers

Jahr   [The king of Upper and Lower Egypt *Wsr-kaf*   **No. 3**
x+3   donated as his memorial to:]

> [God --------:] on farmland 1700 acres in the
>   North country.
>   Remainer destroyed.

  Nile height: destroyed

King Sahurea.

Year   The heading has not survived, but can be deduced
X+1   from the annual notations.

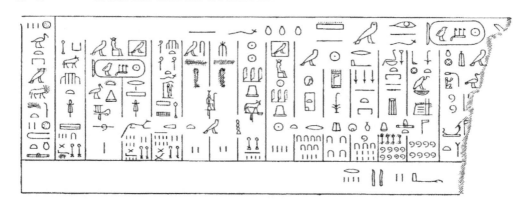

34

a) The king of Upper and Lower Egypt Sahurea donated as his memorial to:
-------in Heliopolis --------------------200 ------

Nkhbt, the lady of the *Pr-wr*	sacrificial rations daily:				800
Buto, the ladt of the *Pr-nsr*...................	"	"	"	:	4800
Rea in the *Snwt* house	"	"	"	:	138
Rea in the *Ntri* (house) of the south ...	"	"	"	:	40
Rea in *Tp-ht*	"	"	"	:	74
Hathor in the Sun Temple *Skht-Rea* ...	"	"	"	:	4
Rea from Skht-*Rea*	farmland in ---- district .. 2000 acres				
Ms	"	" Busiris district ... 2	"		
Sm	"	" Busiris district ... 2	"		
Khnt-tawtf.......................................	"	" Memphis dist. 2	"		
Hathor in the *R-sh* of the *Sahurea* ..	"	" ---- district 2	"		
" " " Temple of Pyramid					
Kha-ba-Sahurea	"	" Libya district 1	"		
the white bull	"	" Tanis district 13	"		

b) 3rd time of finding ----------.
The year after the 2nd time of payment.

Nile height: 2 cubits, 2 ¼ fingers.

Year
x+2

The king of Upper and Lower Egypt
Sahurea donated as his memorial to:
The renewal of the gods --------
Remainder destroyed

Nile height: Not preserved.

No. 2

Since there are years of Sahurea here as well as in the previous line, the line has no special header.

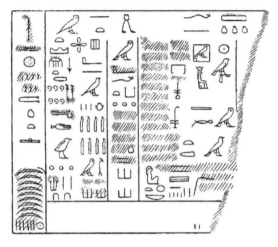

a) [King of Upper and Lower Egypt *Sahurea* donated as]
his memorial to:

> *Rea*----   farmland in the north and south country ---- morning
> *Hathor*   "   " " "   "   "   "   ----   "
> -----------   "   " " "   "   "   "   ----   "

------------------------------------ all things.

what was brought

> from *Mfkat* country: ----- (product) ----- (number)
> from *Pwnt*: Myrrhen 80000' --- (product) --- (number);
>   --- (product, namely Holzer) 2900; ---(product)
>   --- (number)

b) 6th (?) time of the count.

> The number is not certain. According to Manetho, Sahure reigned 13
> years, according to the Turin Papyrus 12 years. The reading 6th
> time would go well with this if the censuses took place every two
> years (Sethe).

Nile height: Destroyed

Year 13(?). 9 months, 6 days.   **No. 2**

> The last incomplete year of the king.
> The number of months and days is quite uncertain.
> This incomplete year has squeezed into the space of
> the previous year.
> So here too, as in obverse, line 5, no. 7, there is an
> oversight that was noticed later.

King Nefer-er-ke-rea.

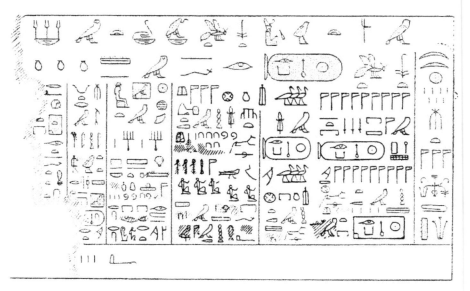

Since the special stripe for the heading is missing, this has been moved down into the space for the yearly notations.

Year 1.   **No. 3**

a) 2nd month, 7th day.

   Birth of the gods.

   Unification of the two countries.

   Moving around the wall.

b) King of Upper and Lower Egypt *Nefer-er-ke-rea* donated as his memorial for:

   The ninth of gods: --- acres of farmland in ---, in the area of the city "*Nefer-er-ke-rea* loved by the ninth of the gods," in the Memphis district --------------

   The spirits of Heliopolis and the gods of Babylon

   --- acre field in the area of the city "Nefererkere loved by the spirits of Heliopolis" in the east country

[King *Nefer-er-ke-rea*.]　　　　　　　　　　　　　　　**[Reverse]**
[Year 1]　　　　　　　　　　　　　　　　　　　　　　**[Line 5.]**

--- acre field in the district of Tanis --- the two chief priests of Heliopolis --------

Rea and Hathor each a sacrificial table --- sacrificial rations. ------ A granary built (?), equipped with serfs (?)

Form --- electron *Aihi* (the son of *Hathor*), a statue drawn to the house of *Hathor*, the mistress of the sycamores in *Mrt-Snefrw*[1]

Rea of *tp-ht* ----

[1]This translation of "form" according to Sethe.

Nile Height: 3 cubits. Remainder destroyed.

Year x+1.　　　　　　　　　　　　　　　　　　　　　**No. 1**

a) [King of Upper and Lower Egypt *Nefer-er-ke-re*a founded as his memorial for:]

Rea in the sun sanctuary "Seat of Heart of *Rea*"

the king *Stnh*[1] on farmland ---- morning.

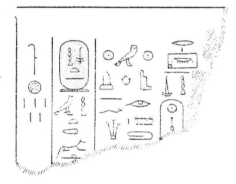

b) year of the 5th time of census.

[1] So a foundation for an old king, perhaps the same one who owns the house, whose official is Meten (LD. 11:3 upper left).

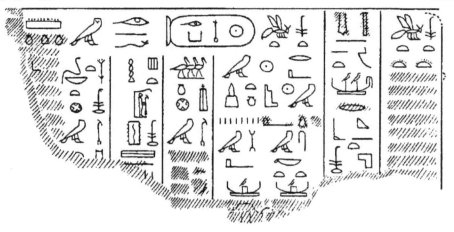

a) Appearance of the king of Upper Egypt. Appearance of the King of Lower Egypt.

b) Walling up (?) the sun barque at the south corner [of Sun Sanctuary Seat of the Heart of *Rea*].

c) King of Upper and Lower Egypt *Nefer-er-ke-rea* donated as his memorial to

Rea in the sun sanctuary "seat of the heart" of *Rea* ----
    Bread
        For the morning sun barque
        For the evening sun barque[2] ----
The spirits of *Heliopolis* ---
Ptah south of its wall: field ----
Buto, the mistress of the south (?) ----

[1]The ship thus lies with *Shsp-ib-ra,* like that in the sanctuary of *Rea* found during the excavations of the royal museums.

[2] So this is a sure proof that there were two sun barques at each sun sanctuary, as was to be expected. In the only sun shrine known to date, that of *Ne-woser-Rea*, only one has been found so far.

It is not possible to say whether there were others below this row and how many.

---

22 [Translator's note: Reverse image for clarity.]

Milton Keynes UK
Ingram Content Group UK Ltd.
UKHW050623250923
429338UK00011B/547